DATE DUE

DEMCO 38-296

SELF-PORTRAIT AS YOUR TRAITOR

SELF-PORTRAIT AS YOUR TRAITOR

DEBBIE MILLMAN

with an introduction by PAULA SCHER

HOW
BOOKS
Cincinnati, Ohio
www.howdesign.com

For more excellent books and resources for designers, visit www.howdesign.com.

17 16 15 14 13   5 4 3 2 1

ISBN-13: 978-1-4403-3461-0

Distributed in Canada by Fraser Direct
100 Armstrong Avenue
Georgetown, Ontario, Canada L7G 5S4
Tel: (905) 877-4411

Distributed in the U.K. and Europe by F&W Media International, LTD
Brunel House, Forde Close, Newton Abbot, TQ12 4PU, UK
Tel: (+44) 1626 323200, Fax: (+44) 1626 323319
Email: enquiries@fwmedia.com

Distributed in Australia by Capricorn Link
P.O. Box 704, Windsor, NSW 2756 Australia
Tel: (02) 4560-1600

Photography by Brent Taylor
Edited by Michael Silverberg and Scott Francis
Art Direction by Claudean Wheeler
Production coordinated by Greg Nock

For Ilene Feinman,
who has always known the truth

Contents

Introduction

By Paula Scher

As children, most graphic designers don't know that they want to be designers. They start out by making things. They are uninhibited and uncritical. They draw from the heart. They draw the things they love: horses, toy soldiers - or conjure up comic-book characters or create paper dolls with complete wardrobes. They doodle in their school notebooks. They make up stories with their drawing, and some of them are intensely personal. Later, when they are in high school, they become known for being "good at art." They draw portraits of their classmates or caricatures of their teachers. They make posters for the school prom or the student-council elections or the football rallies. They have found their position in life. They go to college and become graphic designers. They retain their passion for making things and still cherish the notion that they are "good at art." But then they graduate, go to work as designers, and begin to find themselves far away from the doodles and craft of their childhood. They become strategists, branding experts. They attend meetings. They become planners. They "execute" design.

They stop making things,
and they never totally understand
how that happened.

Debbie Millman is a principal of Sterling Brands. She is a consummate branding expert who has worked on the identities some of America's biggest and most iconic companies. She is a planner, a strategist, and a designer. She spends a lot of her life in meetings, or on airplanes traveling to and from meetings. She is also a popular design commentator with her own radio podcast, "Design Matters." She is a dedicated educator at the School of Visual Arts, where she runs the Masters in Branding program. If that isn't enough, she has authored the books *Brand Thinking and Other Noble Pursuits*, *Brand Bible*, and *How to Think Like a Great Graphic Designer*.

But Debbie never lost her passion for making things. All through that busy branding career, she made paintings and drawings with the same intensity you see in children who want to "be good at art." Instead of taking her away from her passion, her work as a designer had a huge influence on her language-based drawings and paintings. She had fallen in love with the art of the word. In 2009, in her book *Look Both Ways: Illustrated Essays on the Intersection of Life and Design*, she published her literary doodles for the first time. She combined insights about design and everyday life with obsessive hand-drawn typography to create a new form of visual poetry, a 21st-century illuminated manuscript.

Set against her eccentric type,
the essays are a brave, highly personal
form of communication.

Debbie goes a step farther in this new collection. Here, the writing and illumination are even more personal and eccentric. The lettering compliments the message in a way that enforces the feelings that is, each piece of lettering seems to have been created to express the exact emotional subject matter at hand. A designer knows how to do this: to manipulate the visual components in order to evoke the appropriate feeling. It is a planned act. But a fine artist does it for herself, spontaneously, without a client or a brief. Debbie's elaborate doodles have more in common with Ed Fella's work than with editorial design. Though they are illustrative, they are not illustrations but wholly their own. They exist to demonstrate and illuminate, but their complication does not make them easier to read. It makes them significantly more emotionally resonant These drawings are communication from the heart. And they are the bravest, rawest, and most honest form of communication there can be.

better

It is
better
It before
It before
better
better beginr
better before
the better there
before
beginning the
beginning

muscles taut and nauseous belly abeaut abelly aflutter belly abetter aflutter

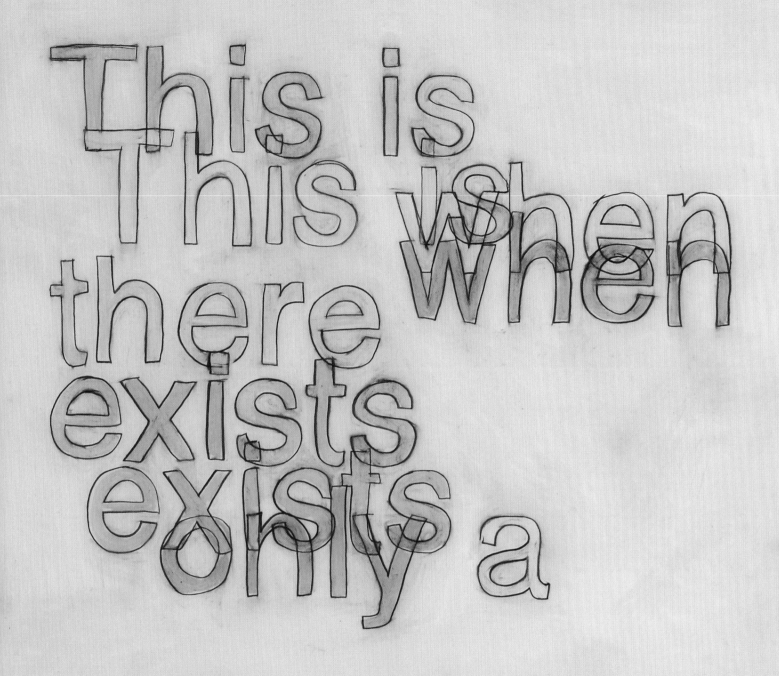

mis-

appropriate;

mis-

16

there is so little to be ashamed of.

I wait.
now wait
for it
to
start
and my
breath

moves
quickly
quick
quick
qui
down
my
back

up
through
my
thighs,
stops
and

settles. It is getting ready to ruin every-thing.

I THINK WE LOOK AT IT THE SAME WAY.

SKEPTICAL YET HOPING THIS TIME IT WOULD NOT HAPPEN AGAIN LIKE BEFORE.

THIS IS WHY
YOU HAVE ME
AS YOU HOLD
ME
YOUR WIDE
FINGERS
WRAPPED
TIGHT AROUND
MY NECK
PULLING ME
IN PUSHING
ME OVER

YOU ARE
TEACHING ME
ABOUT THE
TELLS.

THEY REVEAL
THAT I GIVE
MYSELF AWAY
TOO EASILY.
THIS I KNOW
AND FIGURE
INTO THE
EQUATION

I WEIGH THE AS FRAGILE AND THE NASTY.

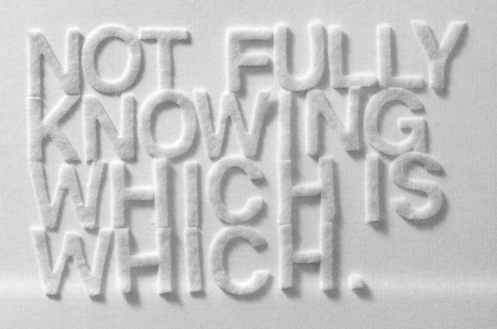

NOT FULLY KNOWING WHICH IS WHICH.

Reflections on a Puddle

Reflections on a Puddle

P U D D L E

One must have a reason for reflection—an eye to admire variations.

And only
so many
days can
fulfill a
day — in
which one
can be
close to
that April
sky — with
sight of it

FULFILL

BENEATH

This requires an understand-
ing: A reason
without, an
inward nature,
a spontaneous
glance.

GLANCE

Post Super Bowl
musings

OR

How I Learned

to stop

worrying and

Love

coffee

Whenever, I tell
people I've never
once consumed a
bottle of beer, I
am met with
shock
and
incredulity

But I haven't!

I grew up in a household that was mostly voluntarily void of alcohol and spirits (unless you include Manisch-ewitz, but I won't) and I simply never developed a taste for beer. In fact, I rather loathe it. I also have a particular disdain for the taste of beer on anyone else. Which, as a teenager growing up in a suburb rife with football parties, made for difficulties.

My parents were more the type that drank coffee, at least my mother was. Every morning she would put up a big pot and when it was brewed, she would pour herself a cup in her favorite corningware mug. But it was the pot that she brewed her coffee in that captivated me. It too was of the corningware brand, but this pot had three blue periwinkle flowers centered on the lower half of the front of the pot, and for some reason, I thought they were beautiful and magical and fascinating. It was my favorite thing in our kitchen.

My mother drank her coffee black. Back then she smoked cigarettes and often her friends from the neighborhood would sit in our burnt orange breakfast nook and talk. They would all light their cigarettes from the same slim lighter, pour their coffee, stir in the milk and sugar and then they would start to gossip.

They would chat about who had recently bought a new car or a fur coat or who was taking a vacation or a mistress or some new pill that had come on the market.

At eight years old,
I was fascinated
with my mother's
girlfriends: to me, they
were magnificently
glamorous with their
brightly painted nails
and tightly pulled faces
and billowing wisps of
smoke, and I would sit
in the kitchen, off by
myself, and pretend
I wasn't listening
when in fact I wasn't
missing a word.

One day, one of my mother's friends, Daphne, the brassy and most confident woman in the group, invited me to join them in the breakfast nook. I was surprised by the overture and suddenly shy. But the women all urged me over and made a place at the table. Then they did the unthinkable: they poured me a cup of coffee. My mother objected, but the ladies insisted and they compromised by filling the mug to the tippy top with milk. I hesitated for a moment before I took a sip, and as my mouth approached the now lukewarm liquid, I inhaled the pungent aroma and fantasized that I had a cigarette languidly hanging out of a fabulously manicured hand and a cute pair of cat glasses perched on my nose. The minute I tasted the coffee I knew I was fooling myself. I knew even before I sipped it that I wouldn't like the bitter, acidy taste. I grimaced and swallowed, and the worst possible thing happened: the ladies all laughed.

"Oh she doesn't like it," Daphne declared.

"Oh give her some time!" my mother retorted. "Who likes coffee when they're eight years old?"

It took me a long time to develop a taste for coffee. Back in college my friend Linda's boy-friend Jorge was CONVINCED that anyone that didnt drink espresso was uncivilized, and desperate to impress him, Linda and I joined him in a Little cafe to become acquainted with this heady nectar. We both had teeny tiny cups perched in front of us; and at that moment I was convinced that what looked like nothing more than two tablespoons of liquid couldn't possibly distress me too much. But alas, even after adding four packets of sugar, I was incapacitated. The two sips turned into two hours before I could finish it off. I finally fell in love with coffee when I fell in love with

Oscar. Oscar
was
British and
Beautiful
and taught me
two things:
how to
smoke
and how
to drink
coffee.

He liked his coffee light and sweet; initially I found it palatable but then began to crave it, and him, more and more. My love affair with coffee and love flourished in earnest.

These days I still put sugar in my coffee but now I prefer it over ice. My mornings mostly start the same way, with an iced grande skim latte and an ultra-light cigarette, and as I put on my black cat-like glasses and wonder how much I have been shaped by my family and my friends and my partner and their tastes. I think our lives are made up of these bits and pieces of our shared experiences and the rituals and habits we seek and feed not only signal our affiliations, they help define who we are, both to our ourselves and each other.

LUCKY

THEY DROVE IN SILENCE FOR THE 25 MINUTES IT TOOK THEM TO GET TO THE FISH STORE. MARGARET SAT BESIDE JACK IN THE VAN, HER FOLDED HANDS RESTING ON HER KNEES. SHE WORE HER BROWN CORDUROY WINTER COAT AND HER LEVI'S OVER LONG THERMAL UNDERWEAR. SHE HAD GOTTEN USED TO DRESSING THAT WAY; THE MORE LAYERS ON, THE LONGER IT TOOK TO TAKE THEM OFF, AND IN THE MEAN-TIME SOMEONE MIGHT COME UPSTAIRS OR DRIVE BY. THEN THERE WOULDN'T BE ENOUGH TIME. SHE HATED THESE OUTINGS, NEVER SURE IF THEY WOULD STOP ON THE WAY THERE OR BACK. FOR A WHILE THINGS STOPPED AFTER WHAT HAPPENED WITH DAVID, BUT IT HAD BEEN TWO MONTHS SINCE THEN, AND JACK STARTED TAKING THE CHANCE AGAIN. IN THE MEANTIME, DAVID STOPPED LOOK-ING AT HER, AND NO WONDER WHY.

Now they were on the way to the fish store to pick up some flounder for dinner.

IT WAS THE ONLY PLACE
IN THE NEIGHBORHOOD
THAT SOLD WISE'S SALT
& VINEGAR POTATO CHIPS.
SHE FELT THE QUARTER
IN HER POCKET.
SHE SAVED IT FOR
THIS TRIP SHE
COULDN'T WAIT TO
OPEN THE BAG, PICK
THE FIRST CHIP OUT
AND PUT THE WHOLE
THING IN HER MOUTH.
SHE WOULD SUCK OFF
THE SALT AND VINEGAR
AND KEEP THE CHIP IN
HER MOUTH UNTIL IT
WAS SOFT AND MUSHY
AND THEN SHE WOULD
CHEW AND SWALLOW.
IT TOOK ABOUT 3 OR
4 MINUTES TO ACHIEVE
THE RIGHT CONSISTENCY

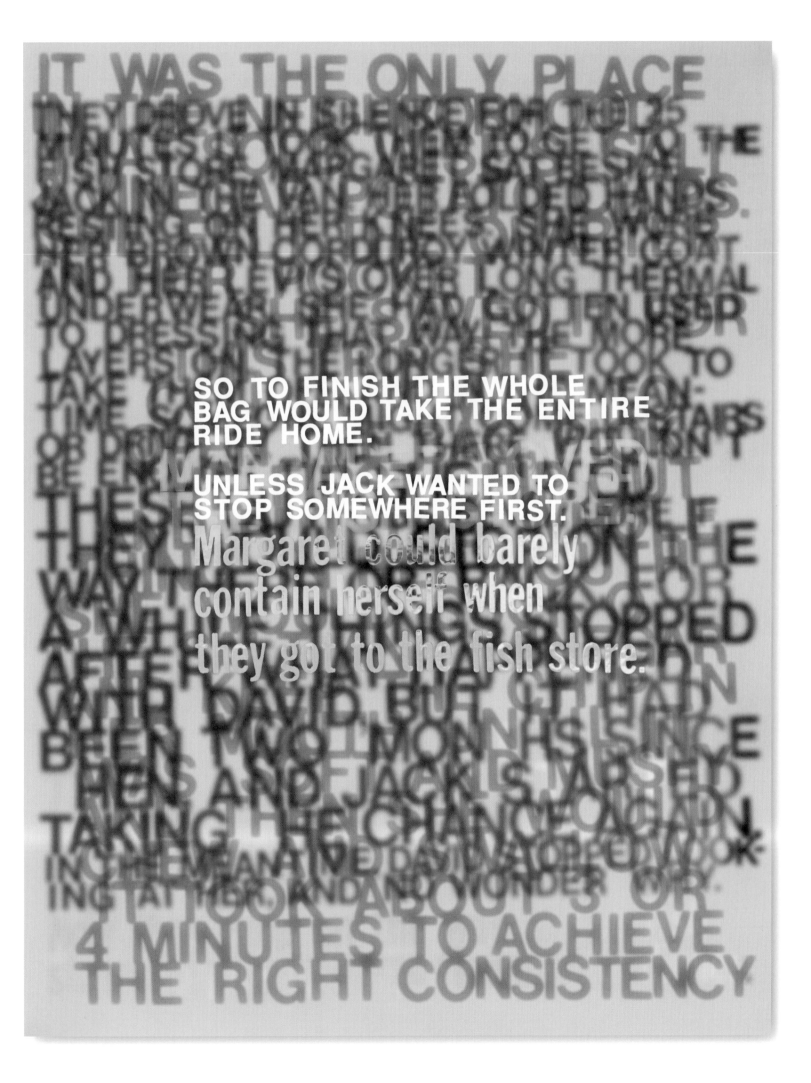

IT WAS THE ONLY PLACE

SO TO FINISH THE WHOLE
BAG WOULD TAKE THE ENTIRE
RIDE HOME.

UNLESS JACK WANTED TO
STOP SOMEWHERE FIRST.

Margaret could barely
contain herself when
they got to the fish store.

4 MINUTES TO ACHIEVE
THE RIGHT CONSISTENCY

JACK WENT TO THE FISH COUNTER AND MARGARET HEADED STRAIGHT OVER TO THE CASH REGISTER. ABOVE THE REGISTER WAS A METAL DISPLAY OF SMALL BAGS OF CHIPS:

barbeque PLAIN, SALT AND VINEGAR.

MRS JOHNSTON, THE FISH LADY,

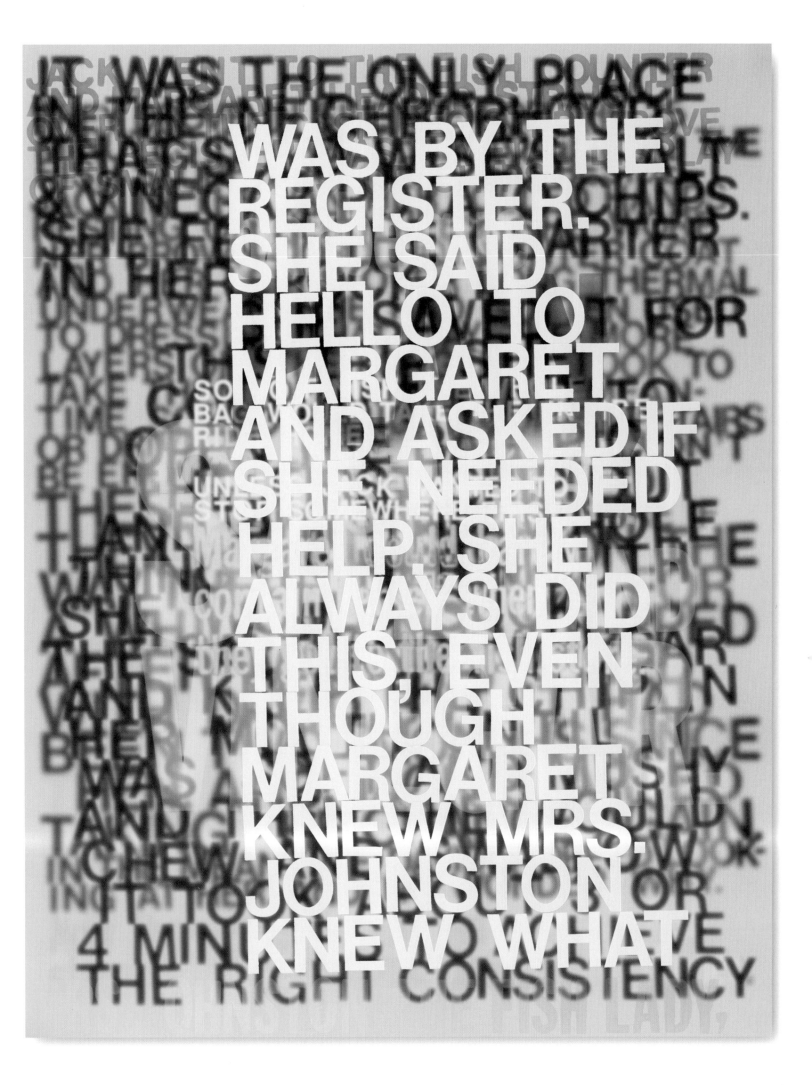

WAS BY THE REGISTER. SHE SAID HELLO TO MARGARET AND ASKED IF SHE NEEDED HELP. SHE ALWAYS DID THIS, EVEN THOUGH MARGARET KNEW MRS. JOHNSTON KNEW WHAT

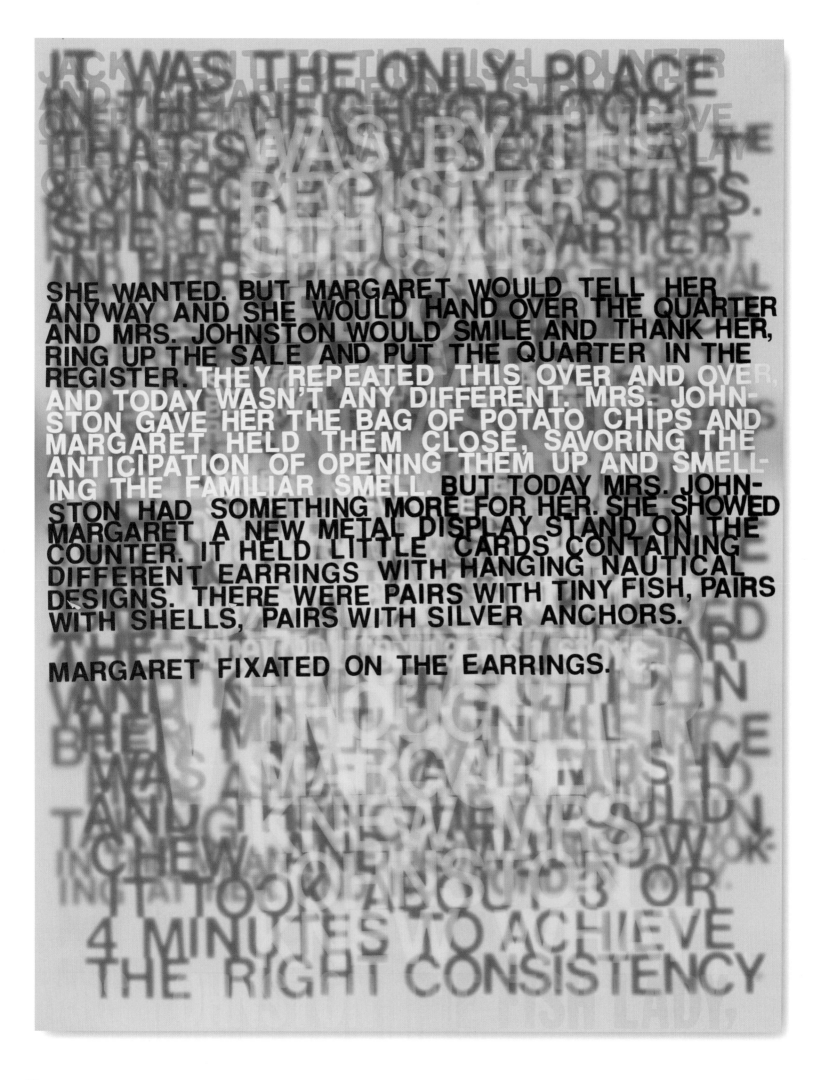

SHE WANTED. BUT MARGARET WOULD TELL HER ANYWAY AND SHE WOULD HAND OVER THE QUARTER AND MRS. JOHNSTON WOULD SMILE AND THANK HER, RING UP THE SALE AND PUT THE QUARTER IN THE REGISTER. THEY REPEATED THIS OVER AND OVER, AND TODAY WASN'T ANY DIFFERENT. MRS. JOHNSTON GAVE HER THE BAG OF POTATO CHIPS AND MARGARET HELD THEM CLOSE, SAVORING THE ANTICIPATION OF OPENING THEM UP AND SMELLING THE FAMILIAR SMELL. BUT TODAY MRS. JOHNSTON HAD SOMETHING MORE FOR HER. SHE SHOWED MARGARET A NEW METAL DISPLAY STAND ON THE COUNTER. IT HELD LITTLE CARDS CONTAINING DIFFERENT EARRINGS WITH HANGING NAUTICAL DESIGNS. THERE WERE PAIRS WITH TINY FISH, PAIRS WITH SHELLS, PAIRS WITH SILVER ANCHORS.

MARGARET FIXATED ON THE EARRINGS.

DESPITE HAVING HER EARS PIERCED 3 YEARS AGO, HER MOM ONLY ALLOWED HER TO WEAR EARRINGS WITH POSTS. SHE DIDN'T LIKE YOUNG GIRLS TO WEAR DANGLY JEWELRY

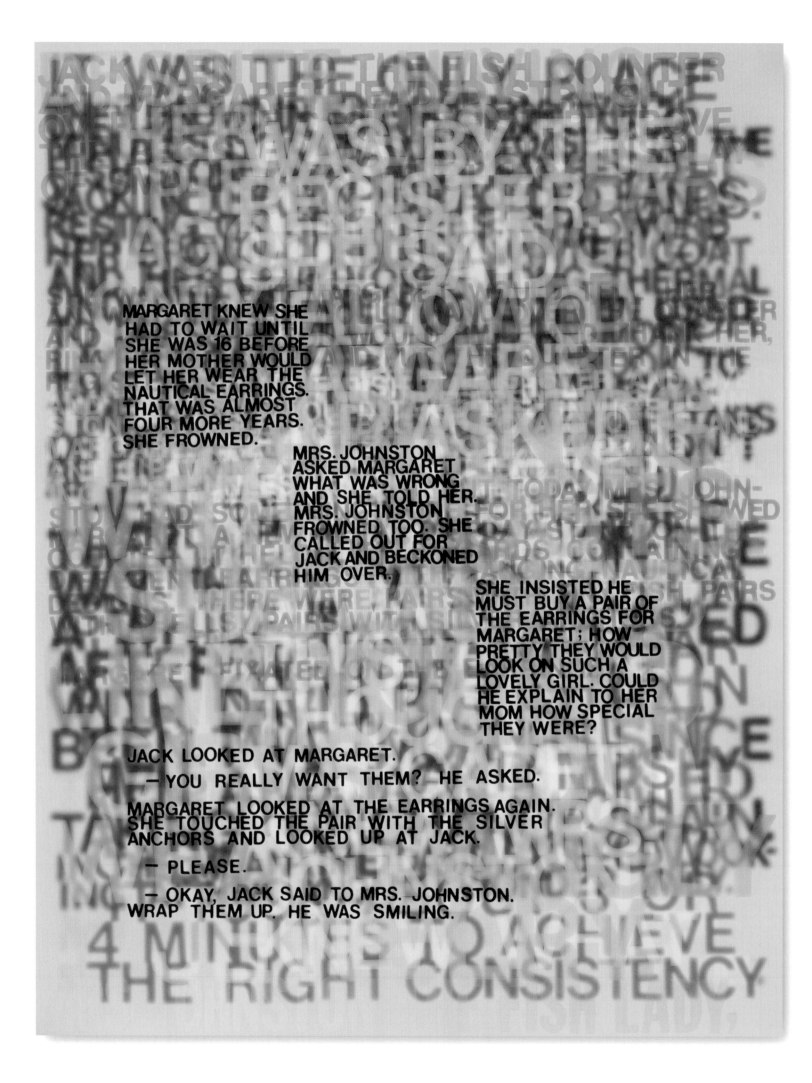

MARGARET KNEW SHE
HAD TO WAIT UNTIL
SHE WAS 16 BEFORE
HER MOTHER WOULD
LET HER WEAR THE
NAUTICAL EARRINGS.
THAT WAS ALMOST
FOUR MORE YEARS.
SHE FROWNED.

MRS. JOHNSTON
ASKED MARGARET
WHAT WAS WRONG
AND SHE TOLD HER.
MRS. JOHNSTON
FROWNED TOO. SHE
CALLED OUT FOR
JACK AND BECKONED
HIM OVER.

SHE INSISTED HE
MUST BUY A PAIR OF
THE EARRINGS FOR
MARGARET; HOW
PRETTY THEY WOULD
LOOK ON SUCH A
LOVELY GIRL. COULD
HE EXPLAIN TO HER
MOM HOW SPECIAL
THEY WERE?

JACK LOOKED AT MARGARET.

— YOU REALLY WANT THEM? HE ASKED.

MARGARET LOOKED AT THE EARRINGS AGAIN.
SHE TOUCHED THE PAIR WITH THE SILVER
ANCHORS AND LOOKED UP AT JACK.

— PLEASE.

— OKAY, JACK SAID TO MRS. JOHNSTON.
WRAP THEM UP. HE WAS SMILING.

4 MINUTES TO ACHIEVE
THE RIGHT CONSISTENCY

MARGARET, SQUEALED.

MRS JOHNSTON
TOOK THEM OFF OF
THE RACK AND SHE
HELPED HER PUT
THEM ON MARGARET
LOOKED AGAINST
THE FISH COUNTER
AND SHE COULD
SEE HER REFLECTION
IN THE GLASS.
THEY LOOKED BEAUTI-
FUL DANG-
LING OFF
HER EARS.

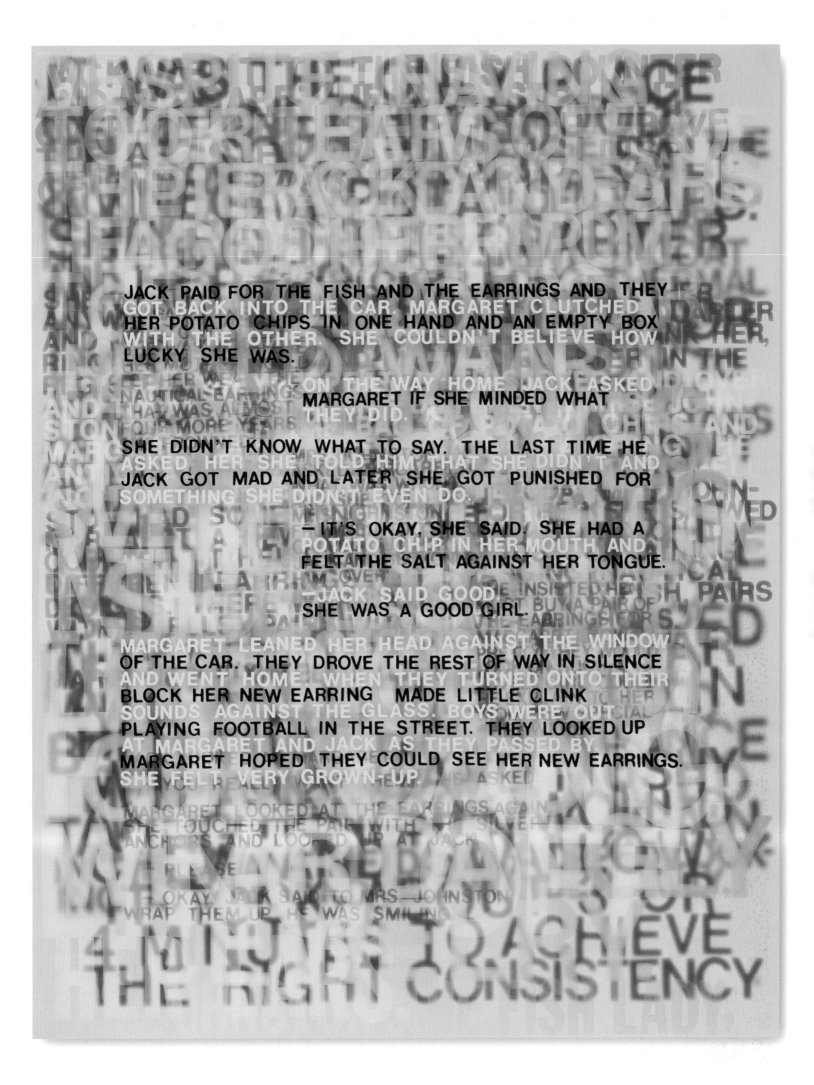

JACK PAID FOR THE FISH AND THE EARRINGS AND THEY
GOT BACK INTO THE CAR. MARGARET CLUTCHED
HER POTATO CHIPS IN ONE HAND AND AN EMPTY BOX
WITH THE OTHER. SHE COULDN'T BELIEVE HOW
LUCKY SHE WAS.

ON THE WAY HOME JACK ASKED
MARGARET IF SHE MINDED WHAT
THEY DID.

SHE DIDN'T KNOW WHAT TO SAY. THE LAST TIME HE
ASKED HER SHE TOLD HIM THAT SHE DIDN'T AND
JACK GOT MAD AND LATER SHE GOT PUNISHED FOR
SOMETHING SHE DIDN'T EVEN DO.

—IT'S OKAY, SHE SAID. SHE HAD A
POTATO CHIP IN HER MOUTH AND
FELT THE SALT AGAINST HER TONGUE.
—JACK SAID GOOD.
SHE WAS A GOOD GIRL.

MARGARET LEANED HER HEAD AGAINST THE WINDOW
OF THE CAR. THEY DROVE THE REST OF WAY IN SILENCE
AND WENT HOME. WHEN THEY TURNED ONTO THEIR
BLOCK HER NEW EARRING MADE LITTLE CLINK
SOUNDS AGAINST THE GLASS. BOYS WERE OUT
PLAYING FOOTBALL IN THE STREET. THEY LOOKED UP
AT MARGARET AND JACK AS THEY PASSED BY.
MARGARET HOPED THEY COULD SEE HER NEW EARRINGS.
SHE FELT VERY GROWN-UP.

I TILTED
MY HEAD
IN SLOWLY

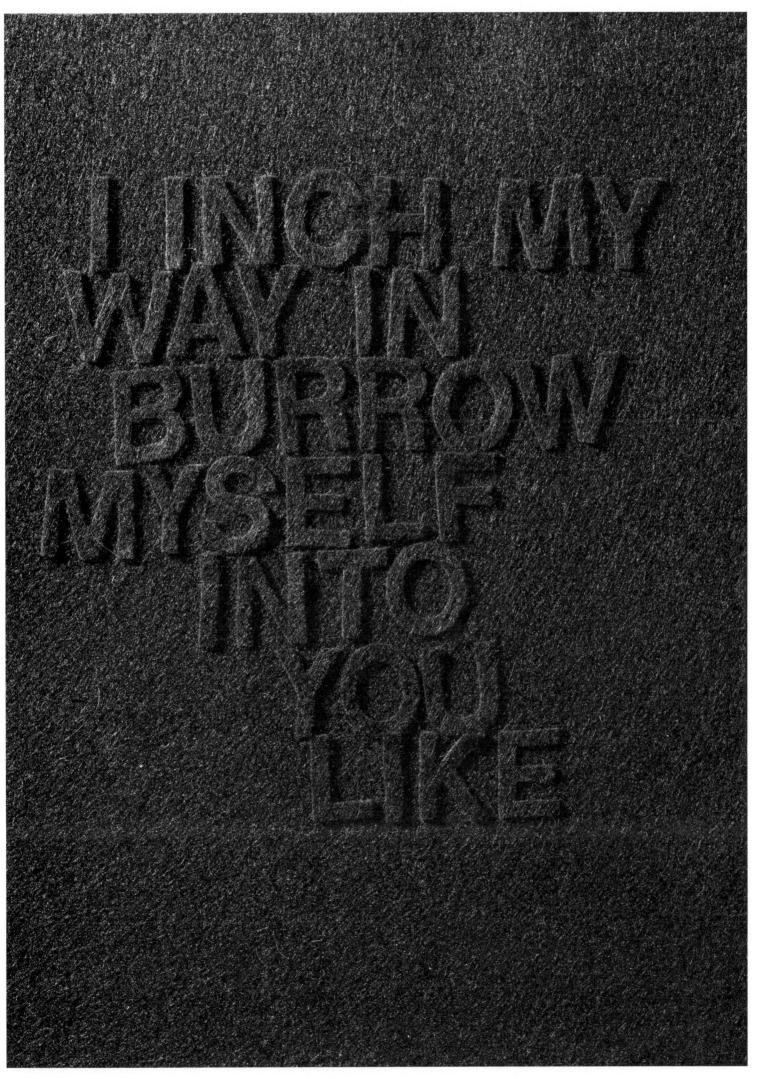

A FRAGILE LITTLE BUG

SOFT
AND
BLACK
AND
ROUND
AND

I FELT
MY
RESILIENT
NARROW
HEART
SHAKE
IN ITS
SHELL
AND

BEG
FOR
FORGIVE-
NESS.

Penelope

...she had
the ...pies...t ...I had

...yellow
...sky blue, some had
stripes, some had geometric
patterns... ...textures
that allowed you to...

Penelope... ...you, me
and when... ...I felt her
squint in an effort to make
sense of... ...that instant,
I knew...

Penelope...
...she...
breezy, ...
...
was smart... ...and
drou...t, on the other hand,

teum doing what
r. paid me $6 an
first job after col-
lege
hour.
My

My first job after col-
lege paid me $6 an
hour.

I was doing what
would now be
considered old
school paste-up and
layout for a fledlging
cable
magazine, and because
I enjoyed
it so much I could
hardly believe that I
was getting paid to do
this magical thing that
I loved.

doing what

doing what

In fact, I never wanted to leave the office.

I was the first person in every morning, and I blissfully stayed way into the night.

The evenings in the office were the best; I would busy myself by drawing picture boxes with a rapidiograph, but it was simply a shroud to eavesdrop on the real designers sitting in the bullpen as they compared notes on the latest issue of the Soho News, or who was going to see Richard Hell at CBGBs that weekend.

I knew I was out of my league and I knew they were better than me, but I projected the fantasies I had of what my life could be onto their lives and imagined that I was one of them, but still me. Only better.

What I coveted
most was the easy
confidence they
had in their design
ability; and while
I worked on mine,
I watched and
waited and wished
for a moment
when they might
accept me.

All that
changed
when
Penelope
was hired.

Penelope was tall and thin
and she had a swingy
brunette bob with lazy
bangs that brushed the tips
of her eyelashes. She had
the coolest hosiery I had
ever seen and sported leo-
tards in fuchsia and yellow
and sky blue; some had
stripes, some had geometric
patterns, some had textures
that allowed you to see
through to her long, pale
legs. As I am only 5'4",
Penelope towered over me,
and when we met, I felt her
squint in an effort to make
sense of me. In that instant,
I knew she didn't like me.
Penelope was everything I
wasn't. She was lean and
breezy, effortlessly chic and
slightly haughty. And she
was smart and sardonic and
droll. I, on the other hand,

was chubby and over-eager;
I bit my nails and wore grey
corduroy gaucho skirts with
matching heels. Penelope
lived with her Italian boy-
friend in a swanky loft
uptown. I lived in a fourth-
floor tenement railroad flat
and had to pass through my
married roommates' bed-
room to get to mine.

Everyone liked Penelope.
For me, her arrival brought
on a fiery jealousy I never
felt before. I wanted to look
like Penelope. I wanted to
dress like Penelope and
talk like Penelope.

Looking back on it now,
I realize I simply wanted
to be Penelope.

Suddenly my $6 an hour job wasn't enough. Becoming a good designer wasn't enough. I needed to buy new clothes and new shoes and I needed a new haircut and new thighs and a new

Everything about me
            was utterly awful
and wretchedly wrong.
            I didn't have money
to buy all the clothes
            I wanted but decided
to buy them anyway,
            and charged them to
my brand new, shiny
            American Express
card. But when I went
            to work in my new
duds, I still felt shabby
            next to Penelope,
and I knew that no
            matter what I did
and how much I tried
            to change who I
was, I would never be any-
            thing like Penelope.
And I hated myself
            even more.

plausible and

could be

When I opened my credit card bill I felt nauseous. I didn't have enough money to pay it, so I asked my mother for a loan. She didn't have much money either, but she gave me what she could after I swore I would repay her. And though I managed to scrape by, I never seemed to have enough. I needed new things and couldn't help wanting more. I told myself that if I could just save $1,000 everything would be okay. I could pay my bills, buy a few pretty outfits and then I would feel better about myself. I would feel secure. I could feel safe! And with that, despite the fact that I still loved my job, I began to look for another one that would pay me more.

Shortly thereafter, I found a job as a Director of Marketing at a real estate company in Westchester. It was a big title with a big increase in salary; now I would be making $25,000 a year. And the job came with a car! Everyone congratulated me on my good fortune and the potential of this prestigious new opportunity.

But after the last day at my job, I went straight home, climbed into bed fully dressed, pulled the blankets high over my head and cried.

I hated my new job the entire time I was there. I hated the work and I hated real estate and it took me a whole year to save the $1,000 I hoped would insure my future security. I thought about the money every day on the long, grey drive to and from work. By the time I reached my goal, I changed my mind and decided that I actually needed $2,000 to really feel safe.

When I finally determined what it would take for me to feel impervious to my life's challenges, I looked out at the long, grey landscape in front of me and remembered the super cute pair of suede boots that had caught my eye in Bloomingdale's, and realized I had to keep driving.

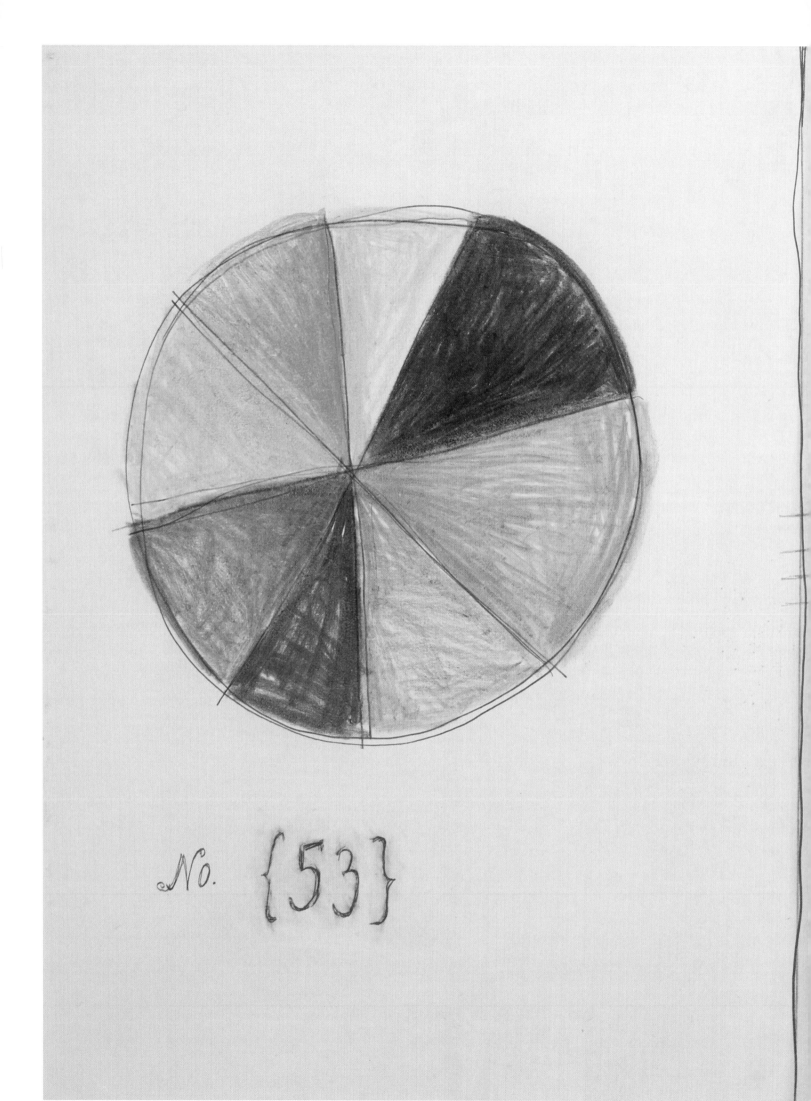

No. {53}

The office is fifty-three narrow steps up on the second floor of a dilapidated warehouse on Mott Street one block north of Chinatown.

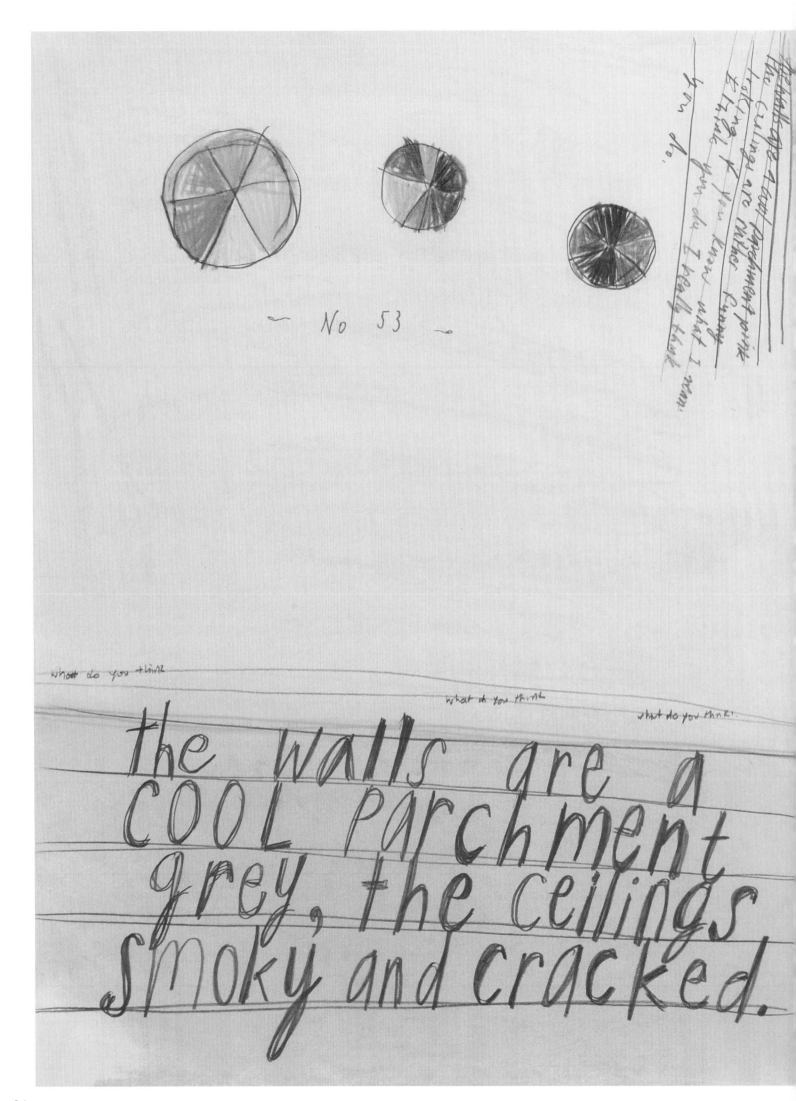

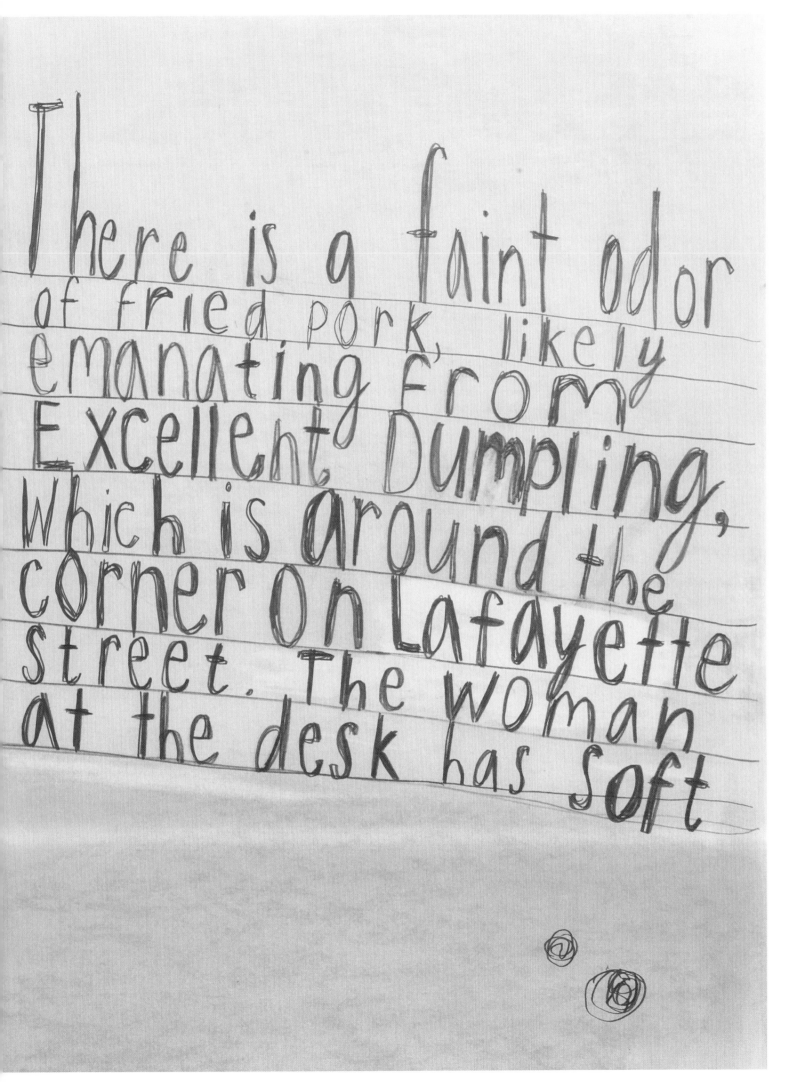

There is a faint odor of fried pork, likely emanating from Excellent Dumpling, which is around the corner on Lafayette street. The woman at the desk has soft

dreamy

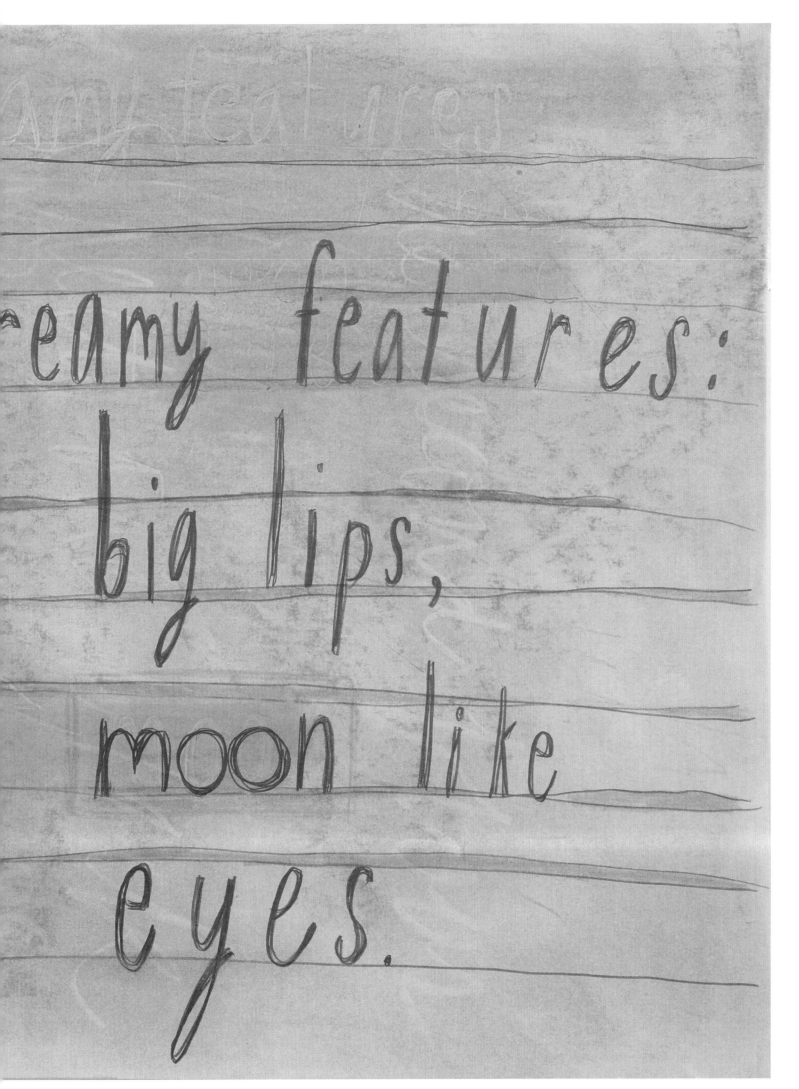

reamy features:
big lips,
moon like
eyes.

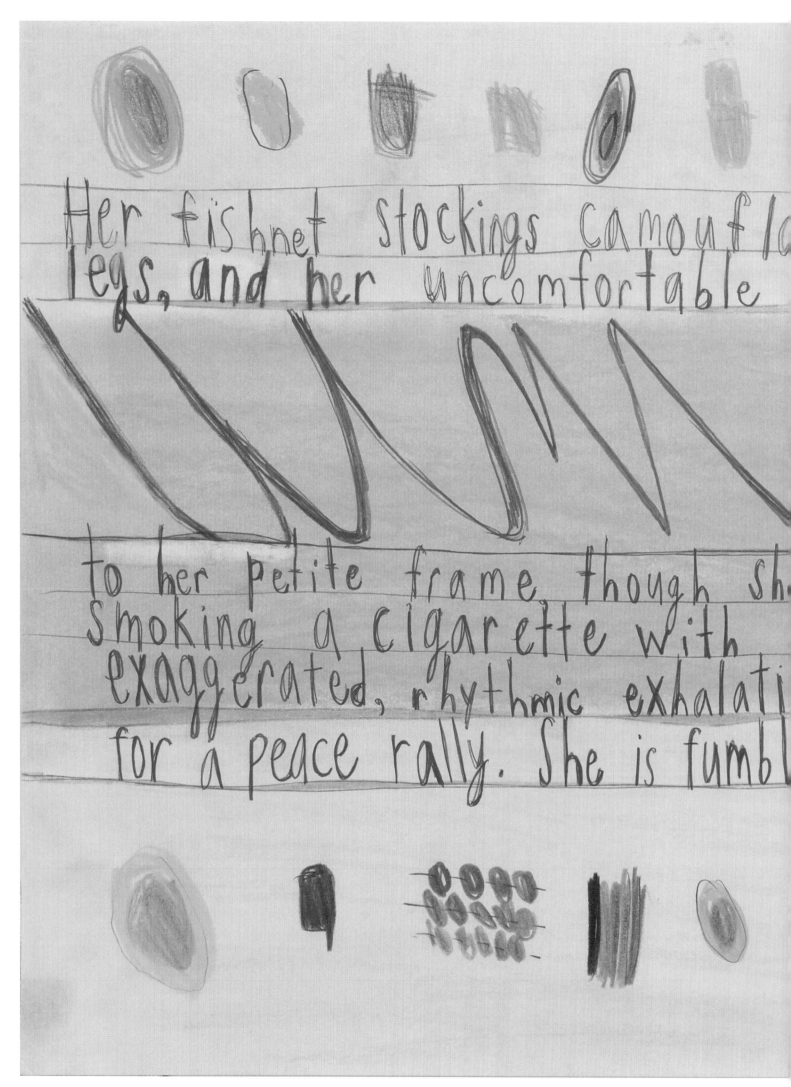

Her fishnet stockings camoufla
legs, and her uncomfortable

to her petite frame, though sh
smoking a cigarette with
exaggerated, rhythmic exhalati
for a peace rally. She is fumbl

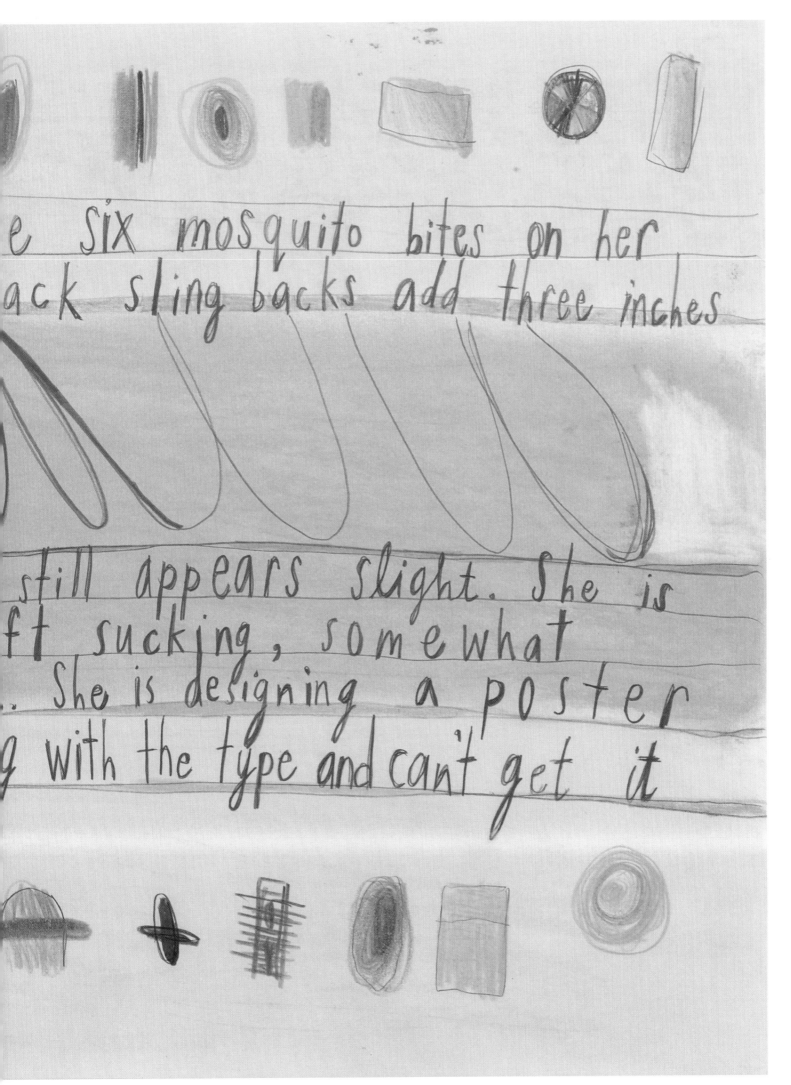

e six mosquito bites on her

ack sling backs add three inches

still appears slight. She is

ft sucking, somewhat

.. She is designing a poster

g with the type and can't get it

right. should it be bolder? should it be italic? should it be red? She gives up and pushes her mouse away. She thinks posters are the cruelest thing to design — there's no place to hide and she has nothing interesting to say.

All sh
to do i
the m
at th
next
how s
abou
shimm

pale skin, that she is afraid if she reaches out and touches him that her hand will pass right through him.

She wants to tell him that the lazy green grey color of his eyes makes her heart ache. She wants to tell him that he makes her happy and everything she sees is sharp and clear and she smells every smell as the air hits her and all this makes her feel as if she could

all they want to know is
she is afraid

possible
po po pop ppps
maybe that is possible possible
make the impossible possible

make the imposs

him this, but she d
down, she pushe
hair from her fac
her email. She

ble possible.

She wants to tell
esn't. She looks
her messy, curly
and she checks
looks at him again.

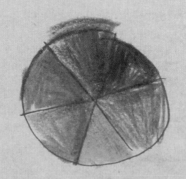

beautiful

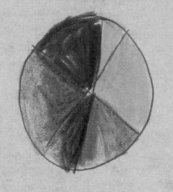

bored

{and}

The man has black gold hair down to his shoulders; he hasn't shaved in several days, his Liz Phair cotton tee shirt is un-tucked. His khaki's are starched, the pleats profoundly apparent. His sneakers are as white as his skin. He is

1441

icon

I worry

diana

time

passes

too

fast

confide

He too

He glan

in fro

and belie

than hers

about the

in the dirt

and beautiful and bored.
struggling with the poster.
es at what is on the computer
t of the woman next to him
that his work is less terrible
and he chuckles to himself. He thinks
night before and wishes he was back
bar with the bad martini's or

Better yet, that he was back in bed with the dirty girl from the bar. He could still smell her sweat on his fingers and he licks them. They are salty and musky and slightly bitter. He likes this and he remembers that this is what she tasted like and he runs his tongue back and forth across the inside of his teeth. He takes a sip of the cold, murky coffee that has been in the styrofoam cup for at least two hours and grimaces. What was her name again? He can't remember. He plays with the type on his screen.

The woman next to him sighs in frustration. She slides away from her desk with an exaggerated motion and

examines a mosquito bite. She loo
up at the man and frown
as she takes in Liz Pha
the white sneakers, the
black hair. She tells h
she feels like going dow
stairs for a Starbucks, an
as she stuffs a twent
into her jacket pocke
She asks the man if he wa
one. He looks up, glanc
around the dingy roo
squints at the curly-heade
girl and says thanks, but no
thanks, he's good.

~ No 54 ~

Fare
thee
well

You didn't realize
I had died until you
walked in and found
me freezing under
the beige blanket
we both hate.

While

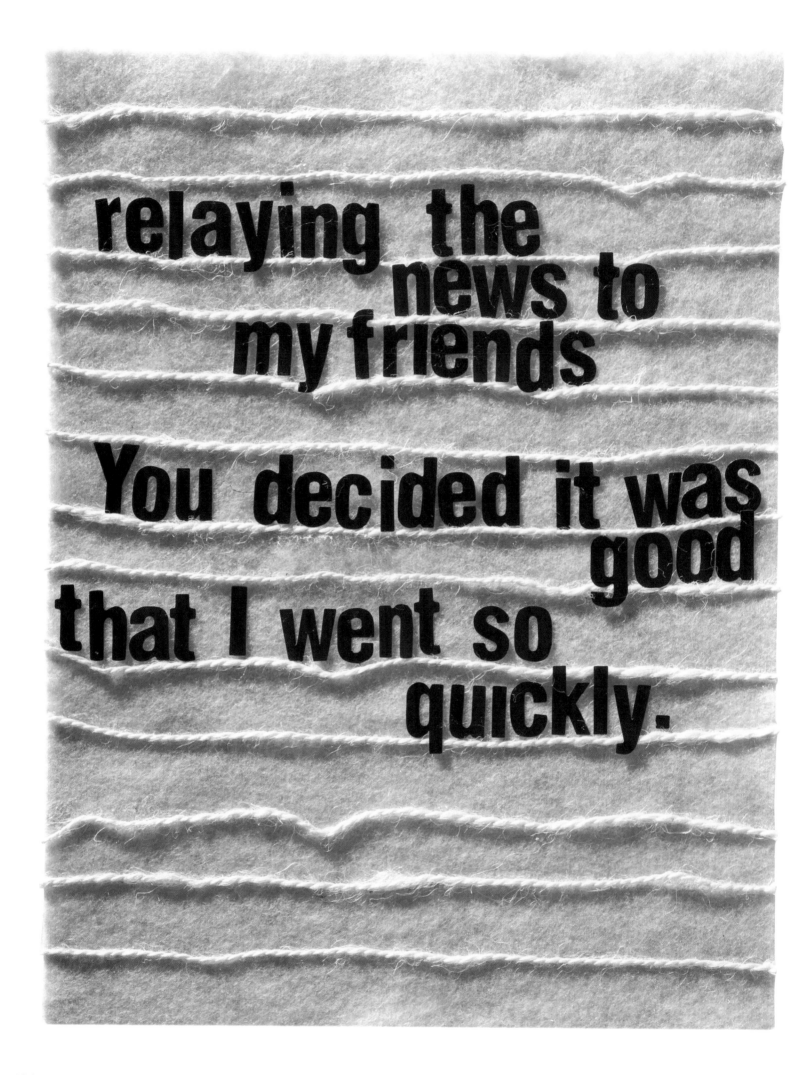

relaying the news to my friends

You decided it was good that I went so quickly.

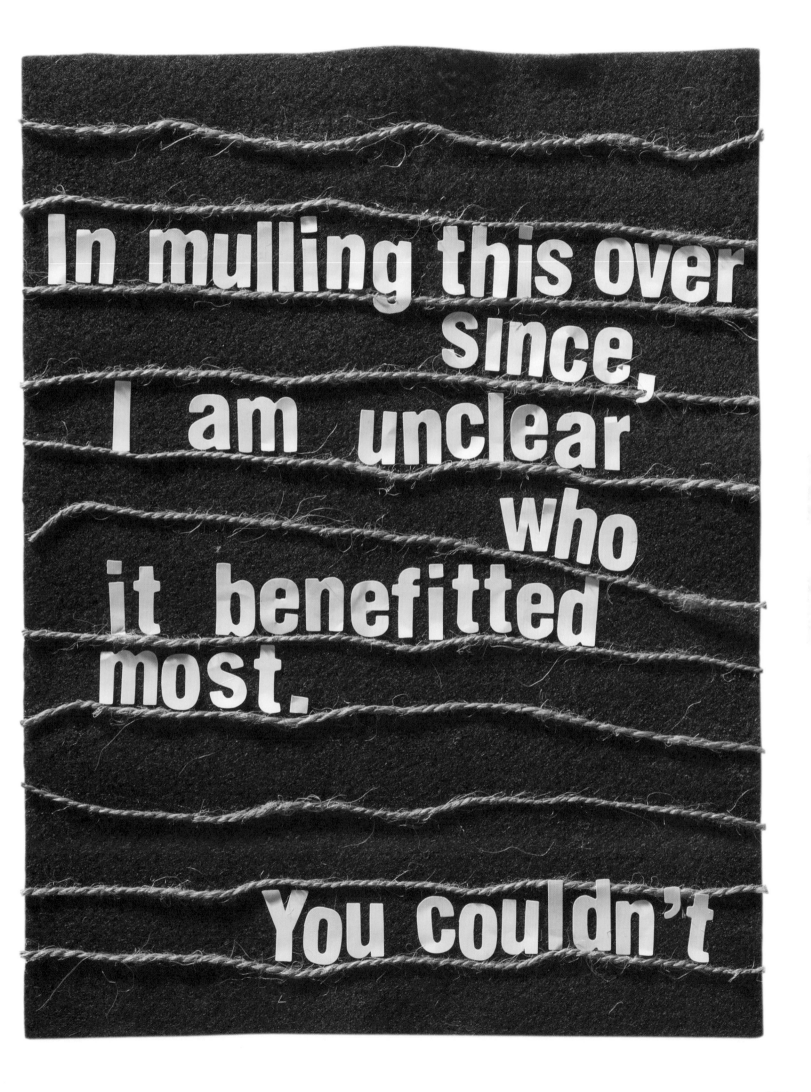

In mulling this over since, I am unclear who it benefitted most. You couldn't know that I woke before I went. It was 2:15 am.

Scruffy was sleeping by my side.

Duff started licking my face. And

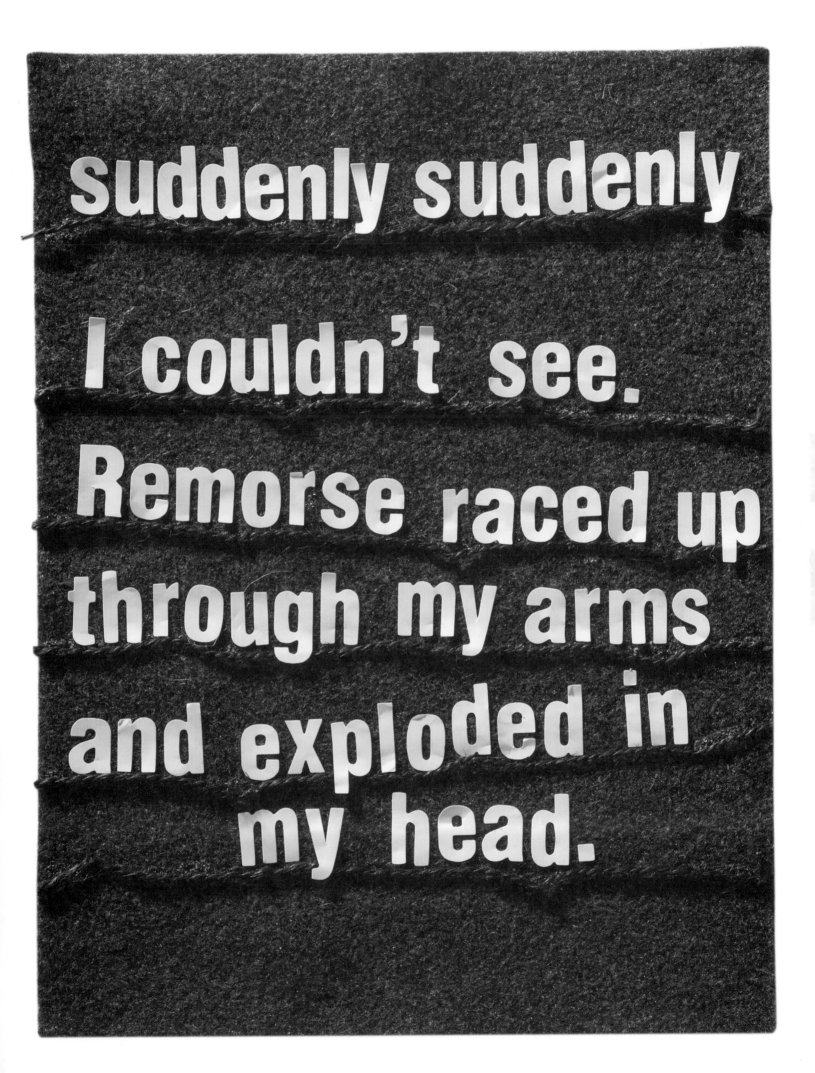

for my brain to
wind down.

And I cried to myself
it was too fast too
soon too too –
I tried to hold on
as I felt the dogs
slip away from
my side.

I have travelled a long way since then – way past Saturn and Pluto.

I like that I can see them up close, but I hate that they wave as I pass.

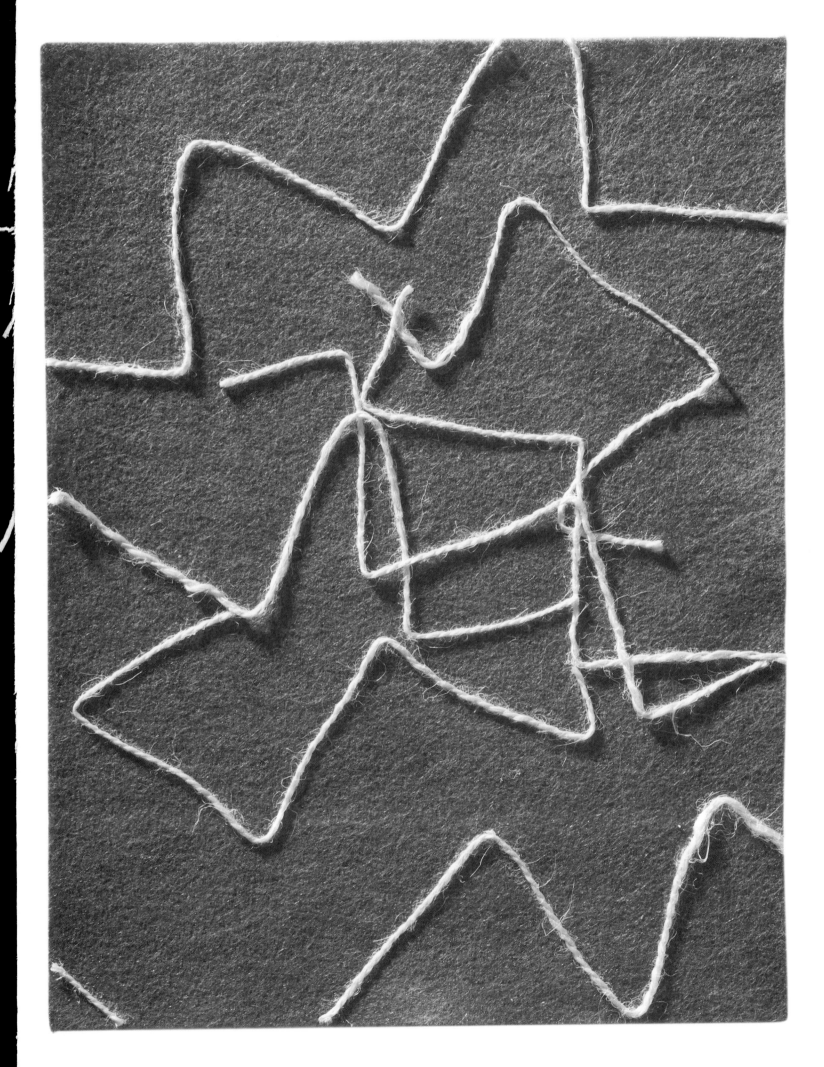

Here we go again:

You're wet, I'm dry and
no matter how hard I try
I find I'm still stone.

I test this seamy side of myself now:
Thighs wide and hips spread
I search you for something long lost.

I lick the salt off my hands.
I see remnants of me in your eyes.
you you you you

you you

You regard me with your pity

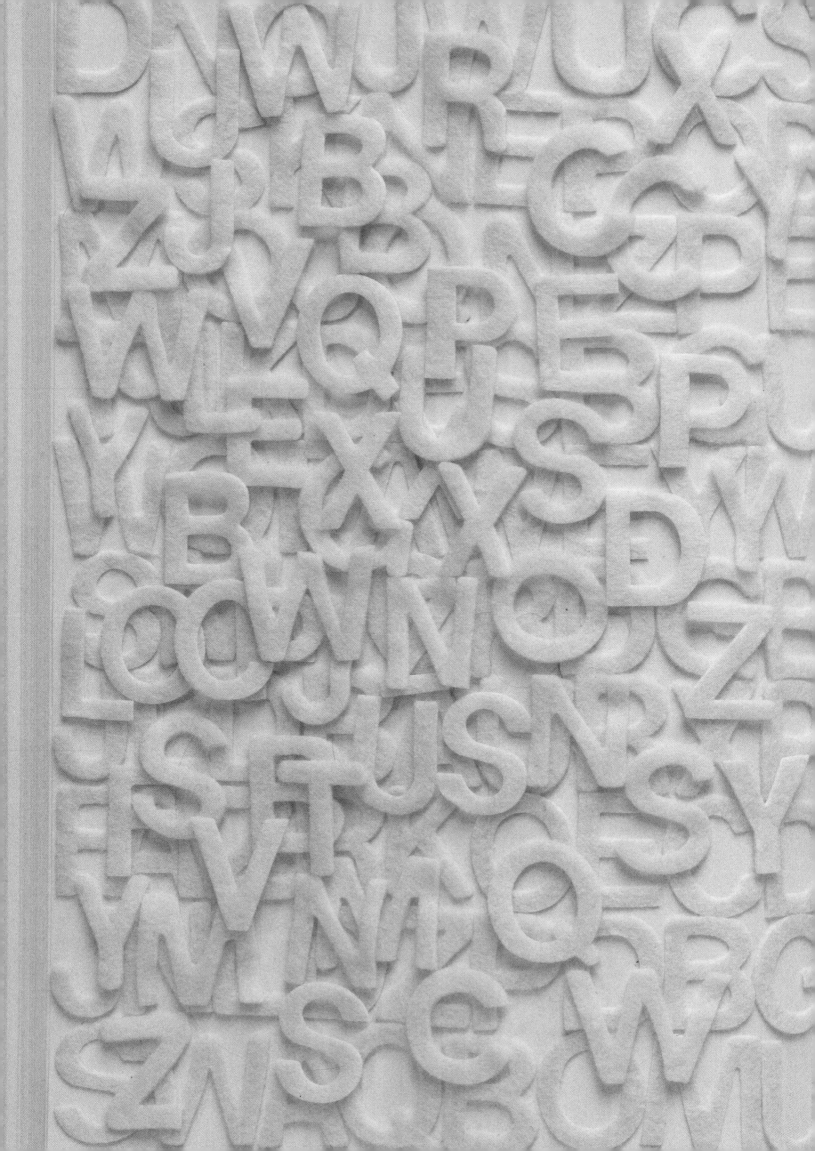